About the Author

I am a 20-year-old college student studying law who grew up and lives in Dublin, Ireland. Since I started secondary school, I've found a great passion for writing as my English teacher, Yvonne Crowley, always inspired me. I hope this book helps someone through their healing process as poetry helped me.

Nameless & Faceless

Courtney White

Nameless & Faceless

Olympia Publishers
London

www.olympiapublishers.com
OLYMPIA PAPERBACK EDITION

A CIP catalogue record for this title is
available from the British Library.

ISBN: 978-1-80439-436-6

This is a work of fiction.
Names, characters, places and incidents originate from the writer's
imagination. Any resemblance to actual persons, living or dead, is
purely coincidental.

First Published in 2023

Olympia Publishers
Tallis House
2 Tallis Street
London
EC4Y 0AB

Printed in Great Britain

Dedication

To Patricia & Tommy

Acknowledgements

Thank you to my boyfriend Fionn, my best friend Leah, my father, my grandparents and all my family for the support and opinions throughout this process.

My Shadow Heart

There is a man I know,
He feels like home,
He has brown eyes,
And brown hair,
He is someone I do not want to share.

He likes to cuddle and sleep,
Real close,
Listen to each other's heartbeats,
As the night grows old.

This man with brown eyes,
Never lies,
He also does loves my eyes,
For him I would forever try.

Time stops too still,
Whenever I have him near.

Nameless & Faceless,

Always craving and wanting,
Never given and seen,
Her who I looked up to,
Is now a faceless being.

The past comes back to haunt me,
As it does each dreary night,
Find hope amongst the stars,
May they always bring some light.

For hope is what I need,
When thinking of her face,
To separate my heart from love that I once gave.

So I sit here quietly, along the window pane,
Looking at the stars,
Looking for her face.

Lonely Path

As I walk along this lonely path,
I came across only one dark path.
A hand reached out and grabbed onto mine,
It brought me to places that made me walk the line.

I recognise this hand, I thought,
It looks as though it fought.
For I realised this hand was mine,
Bringing me down a dark path of my time.

It opened up my eyes to the struggles I faced,
I instantly thought this needs to be replaced.
My broken hand led me through,
Until we reached the final view.

It was bright and beautiful once more,
I don't recognise the dark path anymore.
For I was never alone,
I always had my own hand to hold.

A Home For a…

Whose forest is this, I thought
A small cottage lies in the roots,
Derelict.
Small brown wooden framed windows,
Broken glass,
Eerie.

I remembered the door
All boarded up,
I touched the wood across it,
It pricked my finger.
It came rushing back
As I nearly reached it.

There was the small cottage
Beautiful,
Homely,
Once again.

The Soldier Who Forgot

The soldier who forgot
There was once a man I knew,
Strong and bold and a soldier too,
A pint of Guinness in one hand,
His other placed on my heart.
Maisie (ma-zee) had died and he did not know,
Staying up till 3 or 4,
Waiting for her to come home.
The light in his eyes began to fade,
His memory went, stage by stage.
He looked at my face and did not see,
The little girl who once was me.
This soldier who was once bold and strong,
Forgot who he was, all along.

Poet's Heaven

The library is a place
I like to call my home,
It calms & soothes me,
In every shape & form.

It brings me peace of mind,
As time passes by.

I flick through the pages,
& my world becomes blank,
For I reach a state of heaven
Or a place I come to forget.

Everything is silent
& no one bothers me here
For a library is like honey
For a girl who has
Bees living in her head.

The Sun, Moon, and Stars

For I wish to be the sun, moon, or stars,
The darkness in the night,
For it is where I belong.
For they are the centre of the earth,
Always seen, always felt.

For I wish to be the sun, moon or stars,
For they read my soul,
Each one a marking on my heart.
The depth of the stars,
Creep in and shine bright.
They could cut like cold through the night.

For I wish to be the sun, moon or stars,
For the moon is like a guide,
Leading me through the night.
Memories come back to haunt me,
the night it gives me comfort.
This is where my soul belongs.

For I wish to be the sun, moon or stars,
For the sun brings happiness,
That I wish to be.
Happiness to me and others,
My soul it craves to please.

Misery Loves Company

Misery seems to follow me around,
Grabbing onto my soul,
Like a leech.
The dark shadows in the night,
Love to see my tears,
Clinching onto them,
As their lease of life.
Misery loves company,
For happiness isn't invited,
It's pushed away,
Further and further,
Not welcomed,
in the dark shadows of the night.

Cocoon

I have always liked honeybees & butterflies,
Although I have always been afraid at the sight of them.
Maybe because they were free,
Or maybe was it how their wings fluttered,
I do not know.
When I think of it
I only see them when the sun is shining or with butterflies
When there is light.
Maybe I was afraid of them,
Because they only came out then.
Maybe I am jealous
Because they are free.

.

Too Much or Just Enough?

Her heart as beautiful as the riches of gold,
Her mind broken like a jigsaw puzzle,
But her smile always shows.
She sits alone,
Looking at the moon,
Wondering was she good enough today?
Was she too much ?
When In fact to many people,
Who she craves affection or attention from,
She is as perfect and never too much
To her people.

The Ceiling

The tears on the pillow,
The ache in your head,
The beating of your heart,
And the crackle of your voice.
How do You breathe in without feeling hurt?
How do You feel happiness when the mind is broken?
4 am and the only thing you see,
Is the ceiling.

Borrowed Thoughts

Can I borrow a thought?
For I have none of my own.
They are stolen and robbed,
From the mind I call my home.
Can I borrow a thought ?
A penny for one or two,
I can repay them back in thousands,
Once I find my own.
For these are only,
Borrowed thoughts.

Confused by Deception

Blessings come and go,
The highs and the lows,
I cover my face,
To hide from the blows.
Me and my heart are all alone,
On the darkest of days,
I am barely home.
Broken down like pieces of glass,
The room moves slowly,
As time will pass.
The ticking of the clock moves slow,
Is this hell?
Is this home?

Vessels of the Heart

As I feel the strings of my heart break,
One by one,
I stop and sit, still.
I feel the blood run wild,
Through the vessels of my heart.
My thoughts are not my own,
Merely just a stance in the station.
My heart skips a beat,
As the words trickle through my body.
I sit here, still again,
Listening to beats,
Listening to the blood run,
Through the vessels of my heart.

Eulogy of a Honeybee

Kind people are the souls,
Who experience the toughest times,
For they give to receive.
They are the souls who
Crave peace,
Smiles & happiness.
Alone dragging themselves
From deep sorrows,
Insecurities & hurt.
They are the souls who
Soften the world,
With hearts full of love & soft kindness,
While they alone,
Suffer.

Her Coat

I see her coat on the stairs,
As red as the lipstick she wore.
Her glasses sit softly on her cheeks,
They are no use to her.
Her hands as soft as cotton wool,
A gold ring placed on her finger,
A soft scarf around her neck,
To shield her.
Now her coat sits empty and has no use,
Just like the glasses that sat softly on her cheeks.
I see her hands along the dado rail,
Being her guide.
She never complained or once spoke out,
Her life was content in her red coat.

The Tangled Forest I Call Home

I ran through the forest,
Fighting all my obstacles
Until I reached my safe place.
The tree with the tangled branches,
As I sat under,
It's arms reached out and hugged me,
Like a mother comforting their child.
There I lay,
In the tangled forest,
Looking deep into the night and it's shadows,
This is where home is.

My Eternal Home

I walked to the forest
And what did I see?
A great big oak tree
Staring at me.
I admired its structure & all its might,
I wrapped my arms around it &
Hugged it tight.

This big old oak tree
Became my new best friend
We would laugh and play
Until nights on end.

I finally found why we couldn't be apart,
For this is my heaven & part of my heart.
I was always afraid of death & to die
But this this great old oak tree,
A best friend of mine,
Wrapped it's branches around
& welcomed me home
To the beautiful, dark forest
I now call my home.

Red Clouds

I see the clouds,
Red skies Shephard's delight,
A story I was always told.

The beauty of the shades,
Shadows that follow through,
A painting in a dark canvas or room.

The strokes of the brush,
Different shades of red and orange,
I see the angels painting the skies.

Headlights in The Night

I see the moon,
Blooming through,
The dark night view.

It is like a guide,
Leading me through,
A map connecting in a queue.

A deep look at the view,
A deep breathe, one & two,
This is my favourite new.

Beneath the Blanket

I watched the flower bloom
Through the thick snow,
Amazed,
I watched this flower every day.

Sometimes upright & yellow,
Sometimes slouched & white,

The snow faded a month later,
Still this flower was there,
Fixated,
Every day I made sure it was there.

I built a fence and watered it,
Hoping it would stay,
Hoping.

Dawn

Another day, another heartache,
Time ticks by slowly,
the day drags on,
And we're back in this place again.

I am looking for hope everywhere I go,
But can't seem to find an inch.

Shadowed from the one I call home,
I miss the happy times,
I smile at the thought of them,
It fades as it makes me linger with sadness.

The sun will rise,
And I will try again tomorrow…

The Bear That Comes Around With Me

I have a bear I carry on my back,
It cares for me,
But sometimes worries me.
On certain days it gets too heavy,
It grows and grows
As I get smaller and smaller,
I try to carry it but it gets too much.
I sit it down for a while and talk it out.
I call this bear,
Anxiety.

Brittle Bones

Trapped inside four walls,
Like a prison cell,
I hear the birds talk to each other,
I reach out to touch it,
It flies away, carelessly.

I hear the piano sing softly,
I am dancing in a room full of gold,
Full of love.
The eyes of the yellow, hot sun gleams down on me,
I envy those eyes.

Strange I think or the word that comes to mind,
For different am I,
And that is okay,
For hearts do not break around here.

17 & a Half Wrinkles

A wrinkle for every hand she held,
A wrinkle for every smile we gave her,
A wrinkle for every heartache.

I see her face waving us goodbye,
At the door until we are out of sight,
I see her soft, old hands together,
As she taught us how to say prayers.

Her fingers wrapping around my hair like wool,
As she softly plaits it.
The smoke smoothers the air,
But we love to talk so I sit there.

I look over and see her thumbs go round and round,
Just like her father's would.
I hear her voice in the distance,
That way.